West Country
in cameracolour

West Country
in cameracolour

Photographs by F. A. H. BLOEMENDAL

Text by ALAN HOLLINGSWORTH

LONDON

IAN ALLAN LTD

First published 1977

ISBN 0 7110 0748 9

Published by Ian Allan Ltd, Shepperton, Surrey,
and printed in Italy by
Graphische Betriebe Athesia, Bolzano

Quotations from *The Return of the Native* and
Far from the Madding Crowd by permission of
the Trustees of the Hardy Estate and Macmillan
(London and Basingstoke)

Introduction

As a glance at the plates in this book will show, the dominant features of almost any West Country scene are the sea and the rocks. Sometimes one predominates, sometimes the other, for nowhere that can possibly be called 'West Country' is likely to be more than twenty-five miles from the sea and it is the infinite variety of the rocks of the region which makes the landscape uniquely picturesque, both in its scenery and its architecture.

What is particular about the body of water that washes the West Country shores is that it is genuinely 'oceanic' in origin. It stems from one of the last great eddies of that vast river of warm water which flows up from the Equator and is known variously along its length as Caribbean Current, the Florida Current, the Gulf Stream and finally, as it diffuses into these latitudes, as the North Atlantic Drift. Because of its Equatorial origins and its long track through deep but sunny seas, this oceanic water is at once warmer, cleaner, more saline, and richer in the natural foods of the sea – plankton – than is that of the North Sea and English Channel into which it mingles. Indeed the contrast between the waters is often sufficiently marked to be observable from the air – 'oceanic' water is of a different colour and is invariably cleaner than 'sea' water. Depending on the strength of the ocean current, this oceanic water may penetrate as far east as St Alban's Head and Lulworth on the south coast. On the north coast it usually reaches only a little beyond Hartland Point because of the outflow of the Severn Estuary. Nonetheless, it wraps its warm arms round the West Country.

This oceanic warmth is crucial to the climate of the whole region. The sea has a tempering effect upon the climate of any maritime region because it cools less quickly than the land and hence has a warming effect in winter; since it also warms more slowly, it has a cooling effect in summer. This tempering effect is increased in the south west in winter because the temperature of the oceanic current rarely falls below 50°F (10°C) and there is the further warming effect of the westerlies which have blown across these same warm currents, often for thousands of miles. Thus for considerable periods of the year the climate of the West Country is milder than that of most of the rest of the British Isles.

In January, for example, the average temperature of Cornwall is 45°F (7°C), that of Dorset (the most easterly of the counties) 43°F (6°C), compared with average values for London, the Midlands and East Anglia of 39°F (4°C) or less. Small though they appear, these differences are significant in that they imply a much lower frequency of frosts and snow (at least on lower ground) in the West Country and also because grass and other vegetation begins to grow at about 43°F (7°C), a much longer growing season. And, as we shall see later, grass is called 'Green Gold' in the West Country. In contrast, the south west region is in summer a degree or two cooler on the average than the Midlands and South of England, despite the fact that it enjoys at least as much sunshine and that much of the area is further south.

The price of Atlantic mildness is, of course, Atlantic wetness. In an average year the West Country has a rainfall half as much again as the English national average. Another price that the West Country pays for its mildness is a high incidence of persistent sea-fog around its treacherous coasts – a factor that has contributed far more to the legion of wrecked ships throughout the ages than has the more romantic and legendary figure of the Cornishman waving a lantern.

Exposure to Atlantic current also means exposure to Atlantic gales. At the Lizard, for example, they experience up to 30 days of winds of gale force or more in an average year and many times that number of days when the wind is force six (25 to 30mph) – strong enough to knock up a rugged seaway. For wind and waves are inseparable and gales mean the sea tearing at the coast in its most aggressive mood. Although all waves contribute to the steady erosion of the land by the sea, the great pile-drivers which shape the whole   5

Atlantic coast of these islands are the massive waves of the deep ocean – those great combers which are the delight of the surfer as they heave themselves out of a seemingly windless sea to hurtle faster and faster shorewards. They are a legacy again of the open ocean. Once created by the massive storms and disturbances which march across the wide Atlantic these great waves diminish very slowly; what began as an 18 footer, for example, can still break as a five foot surf in Gerrans Bay 1,500 miles and a week away from the storm that gave it birth.

What the sea takes from one place however, it usually gives back in another, though in greater area and less volume. This means that there are two main types of coast: erosion coast and deposition coast. One of the fascinations of the 400 miles of West Country shoreline is the way in which both types may be found side by side in massive scale and in miniature. Broadly speaking, coasts with high cliffs rising sheer from the sea, where the waves from the west strike at right angles, will be erosion areas – Hartland Point is the great classic. Deposition coasts are usually low-lying areas with sand or shingle banks and in the West Country we have another great classic example in the Chesil Bank of West Bay in Dorset.

Whether it be attacking some great headland like the West Country peninsula itself or a stony spit sticking out from some tiny beach as the tide rises, the eroding action of the sea follows a regular pattern. The sea pounds against any surface across its path with sand, stones and enormous water pressures until flaws in the rock are gradually widened. Such flaws are present even in granite, created by the process of cooling aeons of time ago; or they may be the easily separated layers of slate, as in north Cornwall; or veins of softer rock within hard, as occurs at Lulworth. The result is that these flaws widen until a section of the cliff collapses, often having first been undermined by caves. It falls into the sea and is gradually broken up and swept away. In time a small bay is created and this gradually expands until two headlands are formed. When this happens, the incoming seas are deflected round the headland and come into the coast again some way back from the point. This is what gives so many headlands, great and small, a characteristic snake's head shape. As the erosion process continues, the sea eventually breaks through behind the headland, makes it an island and, one day, collapses it in turn. In contrast, the bay between the headlands is filled with rocks and sand from the erosion process, forms a beach and is protected from the direct assault of the waves.

The result is that in the course of time the coastline is gradually straightened out – only, of course, for the process to begin all over again. On coasts where the sea strikes at an oblique angle, the tendency is for material to be swept parallel to the coast until it finds lodgement against a headland – Portland Bill in the case of Chesil Bank, for example; or on a minor scale, the shingle bank often found against a harbour wall. All these processes are going on continuously and at varying intensities all round the shores of the West Country. They are the explanation of its infinite variety of headlands, bays, beaches, coves, shingle banks and offshore rocks that make it a source of pleasure for almost any activity that requires the participation of the sea.

The ways in which the shore line of the West Country has been shaped can be seen from any map of the region. The whole peninsula was once much longer than it is now, but the sea ate it away and left the Scilly Islands as an undigested morsel behind. But the digestive process is still going on. Legend has it the Arthurian 'shadowy land of Lyonesse' once lay between Land's End and the Scillies. As Baedeker quoted in 1906 –

'A land of old upheaven from the abyss
By fire, to sink into the abyss again'.

There is little doubt that the five inhabited islands of the Scillies were once one and that many which are now mere pinnacles of rock were once islands themselves. But the point about fire is also significant: the Scillies and Land's End and the Lizard are all of fire-created (igneous) rock which is immensely hard and durable.

Although the interaction of the erosive power of the sea and the resilience of the coastal rock determine the shape and nature of the shoreline, slower acting and subtler erosive forces — wind, rain, ice and plant life — sculpture the landscape away from the coast. The, nature of the rock is therefore of crucial importance in determining the shape of the hills, the depth and quality of the soil and hence the use to which men may put the land. The West Country has an immense variety of underlying rock, from the granite of Cornwall through the sandstones of Devon, the clays of Somerset to the chalks of Dorset. In general, the harder the rock, the bleaker the landscape, the less fertile the soil — and vice versa. Fortunately the rocks of most of the area are sufficiently soft to combine with the warm Atlantic rain to produce the gentle green hills and fertile soils that make it the most abundant grass-growing region in the British Isles.

The rock which gives a particular characteristic to the scenery of Devon and Cornwall is granite, an igneous rock which in some early eruption of the Earth's crust flowed up from the molten core to disturb and distort still further the already convoluted layers of sedimentary rock. The heat and pressure of the granite served to alter the nature of these rocks, making them harder and more compact. Sandstone became quartzite, shale being turned into slate, limestone into marble. At the same time vapours and liquids rising from the granite cooled to form deposits of minerals — tin, copper, lead, gold, and surprisingly perhaps, the soft white China clay of the St Austell area.

But even the heat-hardened sedimentary rock (the Cornish generic name is 'kilas') was not as hard as the obtruding granite. It slowly weathered to leave the granite exposed in five great granite bosses which form the backbone of Devon and Cornwall — the Land's End peninsula, Wendron Moors above Redruth, Hensbarrow above St Austell, Bodmin Moor and the brooding mass of Dartmoor. Millions of years of weathering have also eroded the granite itself to some extent, leaving behind a layer of loose granitic sand over the underlying rock to produce a bleak landscape of rolling treeless upland upon which little but heather will grow. These moors are dominated by often spectacularly wind-sculptured 'tors' and a liberal scattering of boulders and massive blocks of granite known as 'moorstones'. As a result of the cooling and crystallising of the once molten granite, these rocks have vertical and horizontal fault lines along which they break easily into natural cubic blocks and flat slabs. Stone Age man made use of these giant cubes for a variety of purposes — standing stones, stone circles and burial chambers which are still to be found on the moors. Modern man has used the Cornish granite slabs and blocks for a host of building purposes from stone 'hedges' and the great houses and cottages of Cornwall itself to the Thames Embankment in London.

On the rocky peninsula of Cornwall, however, the most prevalent rock is not granite but 'kilas'. Granite can usually be recognised by the minerals in it — glass-like quartz, large white crystals of feldspar and shiny black flakes of mica. The headland of Land's End is the only one composed of granite, but the Scilly Islands are made of it and so is the distinctive offshore rock of St Michael's Mount. The Lizard is formed from another igneous rock — a 'schist' (ie layered) variety called serpentine, which is a particularly rare and beautifully marked rock. 'Kilas' comes in many varieties depending upon the nature of the original rock and the extent to which it has been 'cooked' and altered by the granite. The result is that from Watchet, with its cliffs engrained with red and white alabaster, all the way round the south west coast 7 to Berry Head are cliffs of red, grey, black and silver which are the legacy at least in part of what the geologists call appropriately, the Devonian period.

Inland and away from the granite-based moors, the sedimentary rock has weathered in varying degrees to give rounded softer hills, deep river-eroded valleys, green and wooded coombs in which Devon, Cornwall and West Somerset abound. Exmoor, the national park, and the adjacent Brendon Hills, though still barren and windswept in places and with large areas of heath and moorland, are quite different in character from the granite uplands of Dartmoor and Bodmin. The Quantock hills, so beloved of Wordsworth and Coleridge, are of red sandstone, which gives its mellow tones both to the many country houses in the area and to the scattered farms and hamlets and the red, muddy lanes which link them.

The Quantocks are the most easterly of the 'old' rocks. (They overlook the southern end of the Tees-Exe line). Southwards lies the Vale of Taunton Dene and beyond it the Blackdown Hills, crowned with the famous monument to Wellington, which are of greensand, a very much 'younger' rock. East from them, separated by the valley of the Axminster Axe (there is another Axe in north Somerset) are the 'green hills of Somerset' and the rolling chalk hills of West Dorset. Eastwards from the Quantocks lies the plain of Sedgemoor. Known as the Levels, this is an area of sea-deposited clays which was once marshland and prehistoric lake villages. It is still intersected by a maze of drainage ditches called rhines. The area is roughly divided in two by the low Polden hills, a blue limestone outcrop from which, notably at Street, have been dug the remains of many reptiles of the dinosaur type. Further east still lie the craggy Mendips — limestone covering old red sandstone — and the great Jurassic scarp that runs diagonally across England from Portland to Whitby.

The coast of Dorset and East Devon is made of softer rock than the iron bound igneous cliffs of west Devon and Cornwall. Again, the nature of the rock has affected the extent to which the sea has made inroads. The end of the harder rock comes near Budleigh Salterton, with its vivid red sandstone cliffs which run eastwards towards Seaton where Beer Head, 426 feet high, is the westernmost limestone cliff on the south coast. Its stone was used for Exeter Cathedral. Limestone and chalk are the dominating rocks of Dorset. The limestone runs along the coast from Beer to the Portland Peninsula, which culminates in what Thomas Hardy called 'Dorset's Gibraltar', an almost classic 'snake's-head', reappearing again from the sea across Weymouth Bay at St Alban's head and the Isle of Purbeck.

Both Dorset and East Devon produce a particularly fine and distinctive building stone. Portland stone was used by Sir Christopher Wren to build St Paul's Cathedral and has enhanced cities like Cambridge and Cardiff. It is light brown in colour and rough-textured, but in the past was damaged by the sooty atmosphere of the bigger cities. Purbeck stone is a form of marble which will take a high polish, but is not much used for building nowadays because of the small size of the blocks. (Both stones will naturally be found in many buildings throughout the south west). Between Weymouth and Lulworth the cliffs are of chalk, softer again than the limestone of Portland and Purbeck' which serves once more to explain the deep bite the sea has taken from the coast between the two headlands.

Inland, Dorset is dominated by a broad line of chalk downs that runs south west from Wiltshire to the Devon-Somerset border. North of the downs lies the most fertile area, but one of heavy clay, the Blackmore Vale around Sherborne. In the south around Dorchester is Winfrith Heath — the wild heathland that Thomas Hardy called 'Egdon' and of which he wrote:

'The great inviolate place had an ancient permanence which the sea cannot claim. Who can say of a particular sea that it is old? Distilled by the sun, kneaded by the moon, it is renewed in a year, in a day or in an hour. The sea changed, the fields changed, the rivers, the villages, the people changed, yet Egdon remained.'

– The Return of the Native

What Hardy wrote would, until recent times, have been apt to all the upland moors of the West Country. But no more. The 'ancient permanence' of them all is being disturbed by modern developments of many types: Dartmoor by the building of roads and by-passes and the construction of much-needed reservoirs; and Exmoor and the Brendon Hills by the steady reclamation of their moorland for enclosed upland grazing.

But these areas, attractive though they are to the summer visitor who likes moorland pursuits, are not the greatest attraction of the inland areas of the West Country. Put simply, the countervailing attraction is that the area is 'Country' in every sense of that word and what it implies for the hard-pressed city dweller nostalgic for a long-vanished and largely mythical rural golden age. In the first place, there is space – over four million acres of it, nearly 13 per cent of the land area of England. Second, there are, outside the holiday areas, very few people – just over two million, about five per cent of that of England. Thirdly, there is very little industry and few large towns. True, there is vestigial mining in north Cornwall and the china clay workings around St Austell which have produced a new geological feature in the white clay cones, and there is still shipbuilding in the bigger ports. There is also the suggestion that oil may be found off the Cornish coast. None of this, however, serves to disturb the essential 'countriness' of the region. It has an abundance of well-stocked green grassy fields, a plethora of wooded hillsides dotted with peacefully grazing sheep. Away from the major roads and their summer traffic, its hamlets and villages retain their quiet 'olde worlde' charm and many of the country market towns still have a healthy odour of cattle and sheep about them. And, of course, for the visitor there is nearly always and nearly everywhere, cream for tea.

Shorn of the townee's sentiment, however, the West Country is one of the most productive areas in the country, with an output per capita in monetary as well as other terms that matches the best of British industry and suffers few of its strains and tensions. It is a quiet but extremely efficient machine.

The facts tell their own story. Of the four million acres (1.6 million hectares) that make up the total area of the counties of Cornwall, Devon, Somerset and Dorset, over 90 per cent is used for the production of agricultural crops and grassland. At the end of 1975 there were over 570,000 dairy cows in the West Country in no less than 12,000 registered herds – 3,000 in Cornwall, 4,000 in Dorset and Somerset and nearly 5,000 in Devon. Although some of the traditional Devon cattle are still to be seen on Dartmoor and Exmoor and in the South Hams area between Totnes and Plymouth, the most familiar dairy cow nowadays will be the ubiquitous black and white Friesian. Friesians are, of course, prolific milkers, but for the quality of milk needed for the 'cream teas' industry and the clotted cream trade, the soft skinned Jerseys and Guernseys are usually in evidence. In Somerset they still make farmhouse – as distinct from factory – cheese and in 1975, 300 farms supplying 30 units made over 12,000 tonnes. And not all of it would be cheddar: modern methods owe nothing to locality and Caerphilly, Gloucester and Cheshire are likely to be produced as well.

Measured in cash terms, in 1975 the output of the whole agricultural industry in the West Country amounted to between five and six hundred million pounds, dairying accounting for sixty per cent. Remarkably, this was achieved by some 17,000 full time farms and a further 13,000 residential or part-time ones. They employed between them only 20,000 full-time workers, whereas there were over 56,000 in 1950. The majority of West Country farms today are owner-occupied and owner-worked, and the shortage of labour, especially in the more   9 inaccessible hill areas, is restricting the size and scope of farming activity. Rural nostalgia in the towns notwithstanding, the drift from the land continues even in our most rural of counties.

Sheep were traditionally one of the mainstays of farming in the West Country, especially on the chalk downlands of Dorset and Somerset. They have, however, now largely been displaced in these latter areas in favour of arable crops notably feeding barley and wheat. They still form one of the main sources of production of both wool and meat in the uplands of Devon and Cornwall. Dorset Down rams and the distinctive Dorset Horn sheep will be seen in mid-Devon and on the sandstone coastal regions. On Dartmoor and other uplands, Scotch Blackface ewes have been crossed with Cheviots to produce better store lambs for fattening on lusher pastures elsewhere. In Devon, the long-wooled South Devon sheep are most in evidence in the area south of Dartmoor. There is, however, growing evidence to suggest that sheep are coming back to the West Counties even in arable areas and the numbers of breeding sheep have increased by about 10 per cent over the last five years.

Although most people associate the West Country with horticulture — both flowers from Scilly and vegetables from Cornwall — and with orchards — 'Zummerzet where the zider apples grow' — these activities account for only 5 per cent of the farming in the area and fruit for less than 1 per cent. Nonetheless they produce £25 million a year between them, almost half as much again as sheep. Then there is a growing cash crop for many farmers in the West Country in the shape of caravans and bed and breakfast guests. Seasonal perhaps, but significant; as yet, however, the Ministry of Agriculture, Food and Fisheries does not show statistics in its annual summary of livestock and cropping.

If, like the pilgrims of old, we take the road into the West Country from Bath through Wells to Glastonbury we come first to the Mendip Hills, a limestone ridge that falls abruptly away on to the low-lying plain of Sedgemoor. Wells, with its narrow winding main street is built almost entirely from Mendip stone, which accounts for the striking beauty of its cathedral and its celebrated Bishop's Palace. A shrine was established here by Ina, one of the early Saxon kings, and the whole of this matchless little medieval town is permeated by centuries of Christian worship. Glastonbury is the capital of the Sedgemoor Plain, with its drainage dykes and its traditional association with one of the bloodier episodes of English history.

But Glastonbury has a legend within a legend. It is said that Joseph of Arimathea — he who buried Christ — came to convert the English to Christianity. He struck his staff into the ground near Glastonbury and it flowered into a thorn tree. Although the original thorn was destroyed at the time of the Civil War, there is still a thorn in the abbey ground which is said to be a cutting from it. It still flowers each year, appropriately, at Christmas. Joseph is also supposed to have brought the Holy Grail of Arthurian legend with him and buried it on Glastonbury Tor, the steep hill overlooking the town. And Glastonbury became Avalon and King Arthur's bones lie with those of Joseph and, curiously, of St Patrick, somewhere in the area. The Arthurian legend plays a considerable part in the folk lore of the West Country and several places claim association with the 'once and future King'. Legend, embellished by bards and romancers through the centuries and later developed by Geoffrey of Monmouth, Sir Thomas Malory and Alfred, Lord Tennyson, sets the scene of his activities in a number of locations in the south-west peninsula. Apart from Winchester, at least two places claim to be the site of Camelot — Camelford in Cornwall and Cadbury in Somerset. Camelford adds to its claim by the assertion that Slaughter Bridge, a mile above the town, is the site of Arthur's last battle when he was mortally wounded and his enemy, Mordred, killed. Sir Bedivere carried King Arthur's mystic sword, Excalibur, to Dozmare Pool on nearby Bodmin Moor and threw it out over the waters, whereupon an arm emerged, caught the flying sword, brandished it three times and withdrew it into the depths. Whether Arthur ever existed is a matter for debate among historians. Certainly if he did, it was well before the age of chivalry in which Malory, Tennyson and the pre-Raphaelite artists set him. He seems most likely to have been a Celtic British chieftain who in the fifth century fought a series of battles against the intrusion of the immigrant Saxons into the West Country. The Celtic imagination did the rest and he later became the inspiration of King Edward I, one of the earliest protagonists of Christian chivalry in England. King Edward it was who, in 1277, had the bones that monks claimed were those of Arthur and his Queen Guinevere buried at Glastonbury — so Glastonbury has at least seven centuries of history to honour its claim.

The battle of Sedgemoor — it was more of a massacre than a battle — was between the hastily recruited followers of the Duke of Monmouth, for the most part misguided West Country yokels and the Royalist army led by no less a soldier than John Churchill, the future Duke of Marlborough. The site can still be seen outside Weston Zoyland. The battle itself was bloody enough, but the aftermath was even bloodier and has left its mark on the West Country to this day in a plethora of 'mementoes' of the grisly work of the hanging Judge Jeffreys. In this area almost every village has its tale of summary justice and equally summary execution. Taunton in particular, for it was in the great hall of the Norman castle there that Jeffreys held his infamous Bloody Assizes in 1685.

North east from Taunton lie the quiet Quantocks — red sandstone, for we have now crossed the 'Tees-Exe line' and are among the older rocks. It is a place of sleepy hamlets and scattered farms well suited to the dreamy raptures of poets. Samuel Taylor Coleridge settled at Nether Stowey in 1796 and while living there wrote *Kubla Khan, The Ancient Mariner* and part of *Christabel*. Wordsworth too, found inspiration in this the most beautiful part of Somerset.

Exmoor is a national park and many of its wind swept heights, Chains Barrows and Dunkery Beacon, are accessible only to horsemen and walkers. The lower slopes, however, are rich grazing. The heathland has its own charm and is the home of the famous Exmoor red deer, ponies and grouse. It was also in this wild country that R. D. Blackmore set his wild novel, *Lorna Doone.*

The north Devon coast is the scene of perhaps the most spectacular of the West Country's timeless battles between rock and sea. Dark grey rock — the Cornish slate or 'kilas' — forms the magnificent cliffs at Hartland which run north east to Combe Martin with typical bays at Woolacombe and long sand flats at Saunton. Appledore, where the rivers Taw and Torridge meet, is a major shipbuilding centre, Barnstable, one of the oldest boroughs in England once minted its own coinage and was a centre for the wool trade when the West Country's 'Green Gold' grazed sheep rather than cattle. Bideford has connections with the Elizabethan age of adventure in Sir Richard Grenville, captain of the 'Revenge', who secured a charter for the town. It was once the principal port of North Devon, but, like so many ports of the area, Bideford declined in the early nineteenth century.

Between Dartmoor and Exmoor, in the district around South Moulton, is the centre of Devon's famous cider industry. It is an area of stone-built country houses and thatched cottages with the remains of a few old copper and iron mines to remind visitors that there was once industry here. The soil is a puddly mixture of clay and silt known as 'culm measures', which is difficult to drain and to work. As the Ministry of Agriculture says 'small farms change hands all too frequently', reflecting again the shortage of labour. South Molton itself is worth visiting for its unspoilt character and its fine Georgian houses.

Dartmoor is the most easterly granite region and has a plethora of granite 'tors' and pre-historic remains. Like Bodmin moor in Cornwall, Dartmoor was the site of the earliest civil-isation in the West Country. Primitive, stone-age man was attracted to the area first because of the quality of the stone for his various purposes. He preferred, however, to settle on the wild uplands because they were much safer than the deep wooded valleys. He has left many traces behind him — hill-forts, barrows, hut-circles and passage graves. During the Middle Ages Dartmoor was an active mining area and the miners — they dug for tin, lead, copper and manganese — ruled the industry through their 'Stannary Courts' in the four Stannary towns — Tavistock, Chagford, Ashburton and Plympton. They also built a number of the churches in the area.

In all probability, it was Cornish tin and copper during the Bronze Age that attracted the first settlers to Cornwall. Although most of the Celtic immigrants came from the Continent into southern England across the Dover Straits, those who came to Cornwall are believed to have come by way of the Iberian peninsula and Brittany. They were certainly accomplished seamen and brought with them the skills of building leather wicker-work boats (like the St Brendan of recent renown), as well as the arts of navigation and seamanship. With the security and isolation the Cornish people enjoyed from their geographic position at the end of the south west peninsula, guarded on the landward side by Dartmoor and Bodmin and at sea by the west wind, the maritime arts prospered. Fishing became an established industry and as sea-borne trade developed, when fishing palled or did not pay, smuggling and a little quiet piracy were usually available. And when Drake and Hawkins, Raleigh and Captain John Smith were looking for crews for their ships, the little fishing villages of Cornwall and Devon could provide seamen of a skill and experience unsurpassed in the world of that time. Later still, as volunteers or pressed men, these same fishermen manned the Royal Navy's line-of-battle ships — plugging to windward off Ushant to maintain the blockade, in desperate action at Copenhagen, at Trafalgar and the Nile.

Fishing from West Country ports began to decline just before the first world war as the smacks moved to the more prosperous ports on the east coast like Hull and Grimsby. As costs have risen and foreign poachers have moved in so it has become ever more difficult to wrest a living from the sea. Fishermen, like their farming counterparts, have found in the golden horde of tourists a more lucrative trade than the silver harvest of the sea.

Cornwall's isolation meant also that it kept intact its old traditions. The language which is a different form of the Celtic from the Welsh gradually died out, but is now being revived again as Cornwall too feels the same devolutionary stirrings as its other Celtic counterparts. Old customs and ceremonies are being fostered and of these there is none more famous than Helston's Furry Dance which is held in Flora Day (May 8). 'Furry' is believed to stem from the Cornish word feur, a fair or a holiday and the dance itself has pagan origins.

Falmouth is Cornwall's largest harbour and now has a dry dock capable of handling tankers up to 90,000 tons. The Fal estuary, which leads all the way to Truro, is a great favourite with yachtsmen. It is one of the most sheltered areas in the peninsula and palm trees and other sub-tropical vegetation grows happily, including in some places, it is said, bananas. Truro, the capital of Cornwall, is a cathedral city, but the cathedral itself is comparatively recent, having been completed in 1907, the first Anglican cathedral to be built in England since the Reformation. It is built largely of local granite.

There are three great houses in Cornwall which are redolent of both West Country and national history. Not far from Helston is Godolphin House, the home of the Earls of Godolphin.

(The first Earl who served King Charles II, James II and William and Mary was responsible for that memorable advice to aides and advisers of all ages – 'Never be in your master's way, but never be too far out of it'.) The house is partly Tudor and stone built with a slate roof. It has an attractive colonnaded facade added in 1635. The second house is Lanhydrock near Bodmin which is pictured on a later page. The river Fowey runs by Lanhydrock – a river immortalised by Kenneth Grahame as the setting for his *Wind in the Willows*. Although there is no obvious connection between Lanhydrock and Messrs Badger, Mole, Rat and Toad, it is, like Toad Hall, 'one of the nicest houses in these parts'. Cothele stands above the Tamar on the site of an ancient fortified manor house, a superb example of a medieval knight's dwelling. It is of granite with a slate roof and much of it dates from the end of the fifteenth century. One of its attractions is its great hall which has survived intact and virtually unaltered since 1520 and is still furnished in the traditions of those days. It also has a fine collection of armour – but none claimed to have been worn by King Arthur and his knights.

Just before one reaches the eastern frontier of Cornwall, the river Tamar, is Anthony, the finest Georgian house in Cornwall. Of silver grey Pentewan stone, the house, now in the hands of the National Trust, is well worth the brief diversion from the main road to Plymouth.

Plymouth is the very heart of the maritime tradition of the West Country. A major seaport since the 13th Century, it saw the great Elizabethan adventurers embark on their voyages – Hawkins, Raleigh, Frobisher. Drake played his bowls on the Hoe, waiting for the west wind to give him the vital weather gauge on the unweatherly Armada. The Pilgrim Fathers sailed from Plymouth in 1620 as did Captain Cook a hundred and fifty years later. In more recent times, Sir Francis Chichester made Plymouth his starting point when he sailed alone around the world. And anyone who feels that the seafaring tradition is dying should visit Millbay Dock in the August of odd-numbered years when the Fastnet fleet is returning.

The most fertile agricultural region of the West Country is the South Hams, a region stretching from Plymouth to Dartmouth and south to Prawle Point. It has long been rich and carries its wealth with dignity and ease in the shape of elegant towns and superb country houses of which Saltram is the jewel. Saltram has the finest example in the West Country of Robert Adam's interior decoration and also contains a magnificent collection of the works of Reynolds who was born nearby. It is also a National Trust property.

Riviera usually implies a string of jewels and this description is justifiably applied to the resorts which cluster around the warm sheltered waters of Tor Bay – Babbacombe, Torquay and Paignton. From Babbacombe Down, north of Tor Bay and four hundred feet above the sea, one can see 40 miles across Lyme Bay to Portland Bill on a clear day and, nearer, the white bluff of Beer Head. There is then a superb cliffside walk past Anstey's Cove and Daddy Hole Plain to the palm tree-lined streets of Torquay itself, terraced and towered like the Cote d'Azur, its harbour full of splendid yachts. Further south is Paignton with one of the most magnificent stretches of beach in the West Country. Paignton too has in Oldway – now a municipal building – an outstanding example of late-Victorian mercantile Baroque. It was built in 1874 by Isaac Merrit Singer, the sewing machine millionaire and completed by his son, Paris, who was inspired by Versailles. It is set in Italian and grotto gardens and contains replicas of rooms from the Palais. During the second world war it was used – as indeed were most of the bigger hotels in all three resorts – as an initial training school for thousands of embryo pilots and navigators of the Royal Air Force.

The Romans, of course, built Exeter. In its early days it served as a frontier post against the Celts; later the Normans fortified its naturally strong defensive position. They also built the cathedral and the guildhall. The Germans knocked a good deal of Exeter down in 1942 but the cathedral, castle and guildhall were spared and are well worth visiting. A place of 13 particular charm and interest is the cathedral close of which we have given a glimpse on a later page.

Eastwards along the coast from Exeter are a number of small ports of great individuality and contrast. First comes Sidmouth, an attractive town that has preserved much of its Georgian dignity and elegance. Seaton at the mouth of the Axe has red cliffs on one side and white on the other — the change from sandstone to limestone. It is said that precious stones are sometimes found on its beach. Lyme Regis was a haunt of smugglers until the Georgian craze for sea-bathing made it too respectable for them. Jane Austen loved the place and set part of the action of *Persuasion* there. Bridport was once renowned for its ropes and they were used for every purpose from ship's hawsers to hangman's nooses. The town has wide streets and spacious pavements, a legacy of the days when they were ropewalks.

Weymouth is a truly Georgian port. Apart from the dubious distinction of having been the landing place in 1348 for the Black Death, it achieved little prominence until George III became the first English monarch to enter a bathing machine there in 1789. It is still one of the best bathing places on the West Country coast. East again from Weymouth, we reach the end of the chalk at Lulworth Cove, which is encircled by two rocky arms, one of Portland and the other of Purbeck stone.

In sharp contrast to the coastal region of Dorset is Blackmore Vale, undulating dairy country that epitomises the rural West Country. Overlooking it is Shaftesbury, a town built on the edge of a 700 feet plateau. It was virtually founded by King Alfred the Great, who built an abbey on an old Roman site. On a clear day, looking west from Shaftesbury the view extends as far as Glastonbury and its own abbey hill.

There are many who believe that wherever its limits may be set, the West Country is as much a way of life as a finite geographic region. That this is so is to some extent confirmed by what the Oxford English Dictionary gives as the first use of the term West Country — 'Zome honest plain West Country man' — first recorded in 1678. Certainly the pace of life of those who depend upon the moods of the sea or the seasons of the land for their livelihood, or who live in close harmony with both those unhurrying entities, are likely to be quiet, patient and stubbornly enduring. Hardy had something to say about the changelessness of the West Country in his *Far from the Madding Crowd* —

'Five decades hardly modified the cut of a gaiter, the embroidery of a smock-frock, by the breadth of a hair. Ten generations failed to alter the turn of a single phrase. In these Wessex nooks the busy outsider's ancient times are merely old, his old times are still new, his present futurity.'

Just as there is now a nuclear power station on what was Egdon Heath, so the motorways bearing car-loads of free-spending tourists are bringing change to the traditional way of life of the West Country that is one of its greatest attractions. But it still can be felt behind some of the photographs of this book — as enduring, we must hope, as the rocks and the sea.

Alan Hollingsworth

The great west front of Wells Cathedral which dominates the superb cathedral green and has one of the finest assemblies of medieval sculpture in Britain. Many figures have been damaged and others are missing from the original 400 — the result both of Puritan vandalism and centuries of weathering of the Mendip stone.

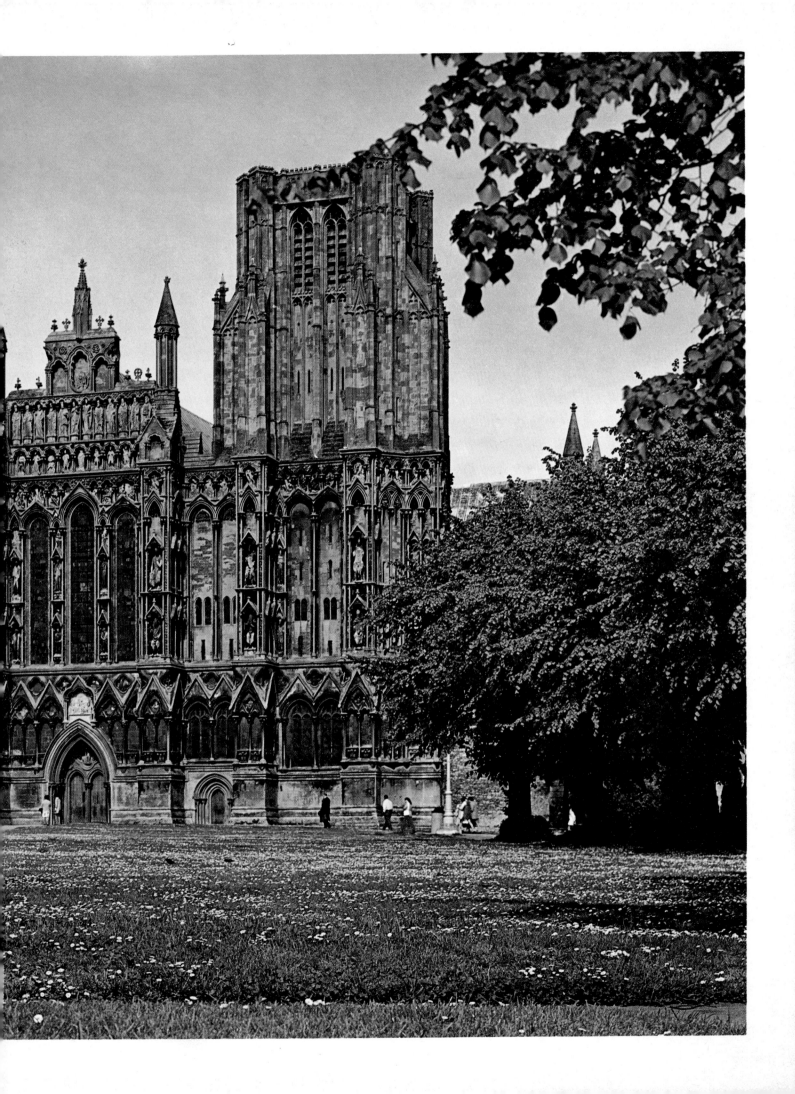

This embattled, moated palace reflects the temporal power and grandeur of the med-iaeval English bishops. Founded by the creator of the adjoining cathedral, Bishop Jocelyn, in the thirteenth century it was fortified by Bishop Ralph in 1341. These fortifications included the gatehouse seen in the picture which was the only entrance. Originally it would also have had a portcullis and drawbridge. There is little evidence that the fortifications were ever tested although the Palace was ransacked during the Civil War. The only Bishop known to have been killed here died in 1703 when the wind blew down a chimney on to him, asleep in his bed.

View from the West Quantocks over the Vale of Taunton Deane. These gentle rounded green hills, narrow winding lanes and the quiet hamlets of thatched red sandstone cottages epitomise to many people all that is best in the 'West Country'.

20

Judge Jeffreys, wreaking the royal revenge after the battle of Sedgemoor, hanged two of Monmouth's supporters in this gateway in 1685. Colhelstone Manor, built in Jacobean times, was once the home of Royalist Sir John Stawell, who after being besieged by Blake and his Parliamentarians in the Civil War spent fourteen years in captivity, returning only to die here. The house is still in private hands.

In Xanadu did Kubla Khan
A stately pleasure dome decree . . .
In a farmhouse near Culbone in 1797, the
poet Samuel Taylor Coleridge was awakened
from an opium sleep — he was taking it, he
said, for dysentery — by a man from Porlock.
In his sleep he 'received' the poem 'Kubla
Khan' virtually complete but by the time
the Porlock man had left, all that remained
is what we have today, incomplete as it is.
But Porlock Hill — seen here across the bay —
has its own claim to fame, summed up by an
anonymous lesser poet:

A novice was driving his car
Down Porlock. His son said 'Papa!
If you drive at this rate
We are bound to be late.
Drive faster.' He did. And they are.

24

Once the family home of the Bluetts, Holcombe Court, Holcombe Rogus, is perhaps the finest Tudor mansion of its kind in Devon. The fascinating name Rogus has nothing to do with roguery. It arises from a Norman Knight, Rogo, whose descendants lived in the village for eight generations.

26

This superb example of late mediaeval
domestic architecture in local stone, the
Priest's House at Muchelney near Langport
in Somerset, is part of a magnificent group
of buildings which include the ancient
abbey, the church and the village cross seen
on the left of the picture. The Priest's House
is now the property of the National Trust.

28

Although it was built on a Norman site, Watermouth Castle dates only from 1825. Baedeker described it in 1906 as a 'large modern castle'. It has a banqueting hall, minstrel's gallery, smugglers' tunnel, wine cellars and a museum — in fact everything 30 a castle should have.

Five and twenty ponies
Trotting through the dark –
Brandy for the Parson
'Baccy for the Clerk –
Kipling's well known verse might have been
written about Allerford a hundred and fifty
years ago. Nearby Porlock Bay was a smug-
gler's rendezvous and pack horses on their
way from the coast to the distribution points
inland must often have trotted over this
bridge.

These seven thatched cottages at Selworthy, Somerset – all incidentally with the typical Somerset bulging bread-oven – were once almhouses. They look across to the heights of Exmoor.

34

Bossington on the edge of Exmoor is renowned for its 'spreading chestnut tree' in the heart of the hamlet. It is famous too for its ancient thatched sandstone cottages, as seen here. The half round bulge at the base of the chimney breast is a bread oven — home-made bread to perfect the traditional tea of home-made clotted cream and home-made strawberry jam.

36

Woolacombe has a magnificent stretch of golden sand, spoil the Atlantic rollers have wrested from Morte and Baggy Points. It looks out across the sweep of Morte Bay towards the rocky island of Lundy some 20 miles to the west — another undigested 'morsel'. As the locals will undoubtedly say, when you can see Lundy it is going to rain. If you can't, it is already raining.

38

Clovelly — a village tumbling down the hill almost like Speke's waterfall — is mercifully too steep and narrow for the motor car. They use donkeys instead and Clovelly as a result is remarkably unspoiled. Three great names have contributed to its fame and its history. The Carys in the sixteenth century built a pier and made the tiny place the only safe harbour in the days of square sails between Appledore and Boscastle. The Hamlyns, as Lords of the Manor, preserved the village for decades from would-be exploiters and 'developers' and built the lovely Hobby Drive a mile or so to the east. And Charles Kingsley, who published his immortal *Westward Ho*! in 1855, spent his childhood in the village. His father was rector here from 1830 to 1836 and Kingsley brought Clovelly and the Carys into his story.

The region round Hartland Point is a district of many 'mouths' — gorges opening to the sea, with their strong-running streams cascading over the rocks under the shade of trees. Speke's Mill Mouth, as can be seen here, first slides smoothly down the cliff into a pool and then plunges to the sea.

One of the few safe natural harbours on Cornwall's iron-bound North Coast, this rocky cliff is none the less a terrifying place for a strange vessel to enter in any but the calmest of weather. Now in the care of the National Trust, Boscastle had its hey-day in the early nineteenth century, when it was a centre for the export trade in Cornish slate. One feature of interest beyond the outer breakwater is a 'blowhole', which, when wind and tide are right, noisily sends spume and spray high over the harbour entrance.

More perhaps by legend than by historical fact, Tintagel Castle, high on the cliff top sheer above the sea, is firmly linked with King Arthur and his saga. Here, it is said, Arthur's parents, Uther Pendragon and Ygraine, first met and fell in love. Tennyson, who wrote of its 'Black cliffs and caves and storms and wind', made the place a mecca for Victorian tourists inspired by his *Idylls of the King*. Even without the Arthurian saga, however, Tintagel possesses a verifiable romantic history going back more than a thousand years. Originally the site of a Celtic monastery founded by St Julot about AD 400, the foundations of which can still be seen, the castle itself was first built by Earl Richard, a younger brother of King Henry III, in the early part of the thirteenth century. Subsequently it fell derelict, the sea ate away the isthmus and separated the main wards of the castle — the upper and lower wards on the mainland, the inner ward on the island.

Once a tiny fishing village, Newquay is now one of the biggest places in Cornwall and the centre for the best surfing beaches in Europe. Some of its combers begin their journey off the coast of Newfoundland.

A peninsula on a peninsula on a peninsula —
the land ends but the granite rocks go on,
as witness the many lighthouses and the
legion of invisible wrecks, to emerge again
as the Scilly Islands, 25 miles out. They
disappear finally into the abyss of the North
Atlantic, a few miles further west at the
300 fathom line.

50

Called 'Ictis' by the ancients, St Michael's Mount was the legendary home of the giant Cormoran, slain by Jack the Giant Killer. It is a 'miniature' of Mont St Michel in Normandy and its priory, founded by Edward the Confessor, was originally attached to the French house. It had a turbulent history in the Middle Ages, being associated with Perkin Warbeck in 1497 and the Prayer Book Rebellion in 1549. It was extensively and expensively refortified at the outset of the Civil War by its Royalist owner, Sir Arthur Basset. As soon as it came under siege, however, Basset surrendered it to the Parliamentarians, well aware that severe damage to it would, among other things, be the ruin of him. He later sold it to Colonel John Aubyn, an ancestor of Lord St Levan, who still lives there. It was transferred to the National Trust in 1954.

52

Carrick Roads is the wrist of a hand of the sea which stretches its fingers deep into the wooded Cornish countryside, providing a day-sailing yachtsman with a superb cruising ground of infinite variety. Since the days of Henry VIII it has been guarded by two forts — in the west by Pendennis Castle at Falmouth and in the east by St Mawes Castle, seen in the centre of the photograph. St Mawes castle, intended as it was for seaward defence, was unprotected on the landward side and fell to Cromwellian troops after only a single day's siege in the Civil War. Pendennis, better sited, lasted for nearly six months.

54

Formerly a classic among Cornish fishing villages, Mevagissey has found tourists easier to catch than herrings. None the less, 56 from above or below it is a captivating spot.

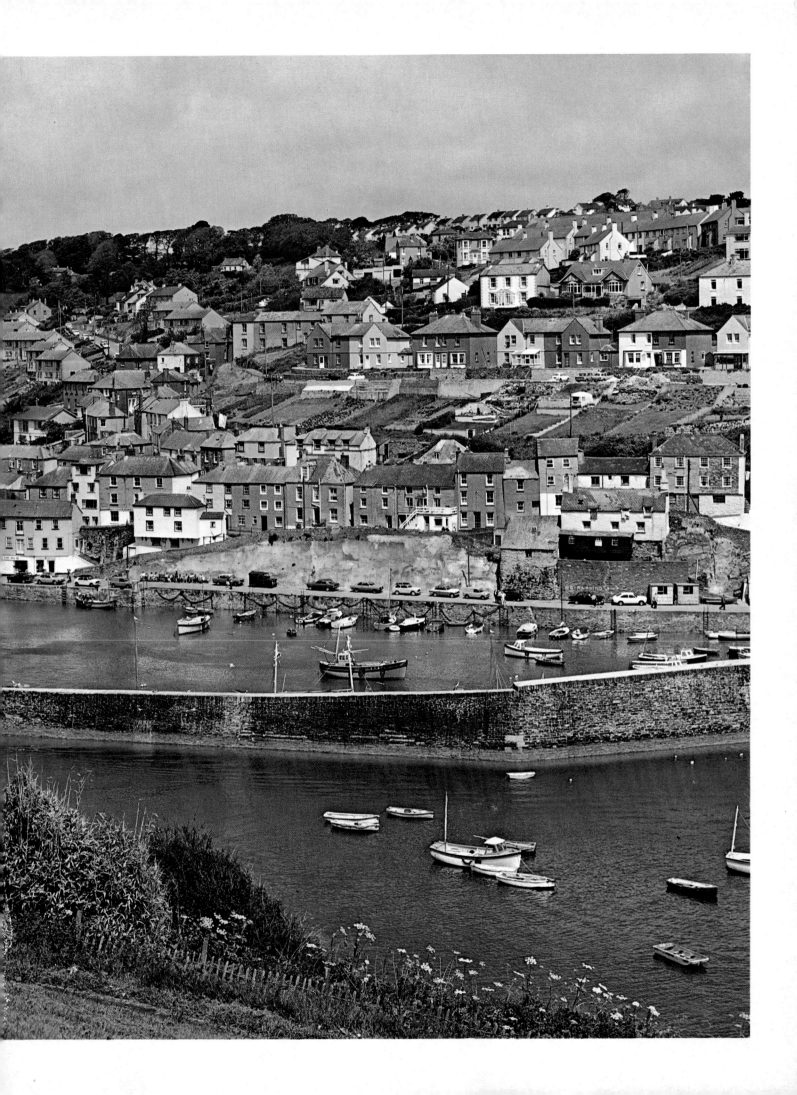

Built by Royalist Sir Richard Robartes, later Lord Robartes, a tin and wool merchant from Truro in the 1620's, Lanhydrock is one of Cornwall's outstanding great houses. It remained in the same family until the late Lord Clifden, a descendant, gave the property to the National Trust in 1953. The disastrous fire destroyed most of the house in 1888 but fortunately left intact one of its finest features – its long gallery in the North wing. This 116-foot-long room, with its barr vaulting and its superb large windows illuminating carved plaster panels of Old Testament stories, is a remarkable example of Cornish craftsmanship of the 17th Century. The house is built of Cornish granite.

Fowey – pronounced 'Foy' – is a miniature Dartmouth in more ways than one. Apart from its physical resemblance to the famous Devon harbour, it is one of the fountain heads of English naval greatness. The 'Gallants of Fowey' were constantly raiding the Normandy coast from the days of Edward III onwards, and the port has contributed its ships and sailors to the Royal fleets since the Siege of Calais. During the Second World War it was appropriately a base for motor torpedo boats operating in the Channel. Nowadays it is an attractive harbour for visiting yachtsmen and has found a new prosperity as the main port for the flourishing china-clay export trade.

60

Though many people feel it a matter for the utmost regret that Polperro did not have a staircase for a main street like Clovelly to keep the cars out, it remains the paragon of Cornish fishing villages.

62

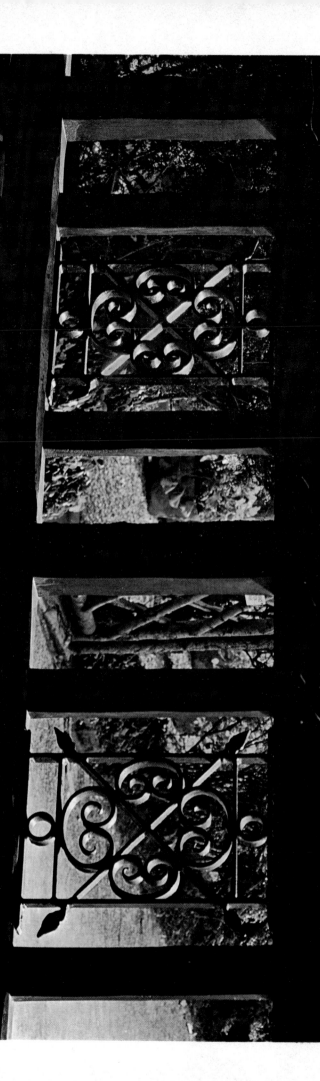

Cockington with its famous thatched forge is a popular attraction for visitors from all over the world. But there is more for the discerning eye than the Forge and the porch — the 13th Century church, for example, or this little lodge cottage with its thatched covered dormer windows and its twisted oak frames. Standing at the gates of Cockington Court it epitomises the popular ideal of romantic West Country cottage with jasmine, roses and geraniums round the door.

64

The stretch of the famous Devon river which
Sir Walter Raleigh must have known from
boyhood. There is a rock in the middle of
the river, Anchor Stone, where he is said
to have first practised smoking tobacco —
in a silver pipe.

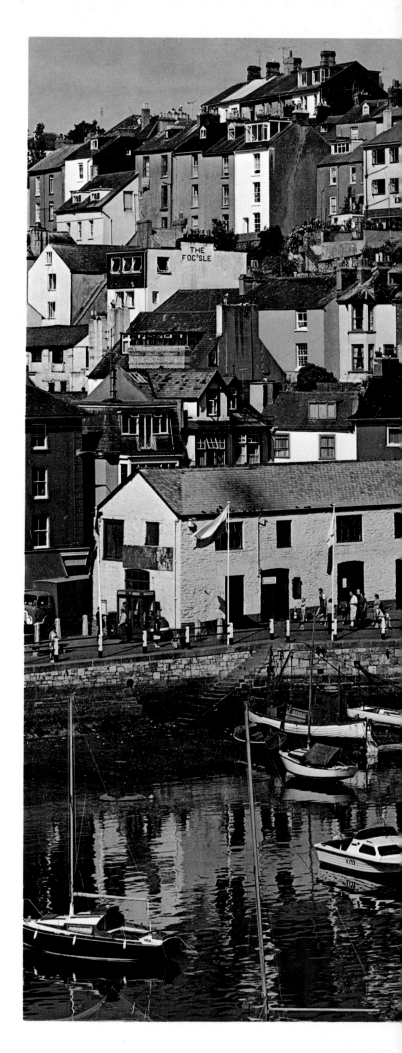

Brixham is a place that has seen much national history. Drake in his ship the *Golden Hind* – a replica of which is pictured here – brought his first Armada capture into Brixham. William of Orange landed here on Guy Fawkes' Day, 1688, consummating the 'Glorious Revolution'. In August 1815, Napoleon, aboard the *Bellerophon,* spent a week off Brixham awaiting the sentence that was to send him to exile and eventual death in St Helena, after his 'revolution' had ended at Waterloo. And it was at Brixham that Henry Francis Lyte, then vicar of the parish church of All Saints, wrote the renowned English hymn *Abide with Me.*

Buckland Beacon, 1280 feet above the sea, stands high above the village. Nestling into its flanks for protection from the Atlantic winter winds are these charming thatched cottages, their woodlands and their streams.

70

Postbridge, with nearby Laughter Tor, is the 'Stone Age' capital of Dartmoor, surrounded as it is by great stones, grave sites and hut circles. Seen here is stone clapper bridge spanning the East Dart river with huge 15ft stone slabs. The bridge is probably one of the oldest man-made bridges in the country and was used by trains by pack horses bringing back metal from the mines.

Not far from Widecombe in the Moor is 'Black Hill', one of the Dartmoor heights rising to 1,300 feet. The grotesque twisted granite rocks shrouded in mist with the wind howling about them make an ideal setting for tales of mystery and imagination in which the region abounds. Not for nothing did Conan Doyle send Sherlock Holmes to Grimpsound, a prehistoric settlement not far away, to begin his hunt for *The Hound of the Baskervilles*.

74

A Dart Valley Railway train approaching Riverford Bridge, near Staverton. This preserved steam railway, re-opened in 1969, meanders along the banks of the river Dart from Buckfastleigh to Totnes. In this picture one of the railway's ex-GWR tank locomotives is hauling a train composed of the 'Devon Belle' observation car and other interesting rolling stock. Open to the public, it operates during the main summer holiday periods and at weekends.

76

Widecombe is renowned for two things.
First, for Widecombe Fair, made famous by the
song about 'Uncle Tom Cobleigh and all',
and which is held on the second Tuesday
in September. Second, for its tall church
built 400 years ago by the tin-miners thank-
ful for the prosperity then prevailing. And,
it is said, Uncle Tom Cobleigh's chair can
still be seen in the church.

A charming Georgian town that has been a 'watering place' since the middle of the eighteenth century, Teignmouth continues to give pleasure to thousands each year. A number of the buildings are of dark red local stone.

80

Exeter Cathedral was established as a cathedral church in 1050 but was extensively rebuilt during the next two hundred years, the west front being completed about 1360. It comprises the largest surviving array in England of a peculiarly elongated style of fourteenth century sculpture. On the west front shown here, there are nearly 70 figures arranged in three rows – angels, apostles, soldiers, priests and kings. Visitors may be able to pick out King Alfred, King Canute, William the Conqueror and Ethelbert, the first English Christian king. The stone came from Beer Head.

82

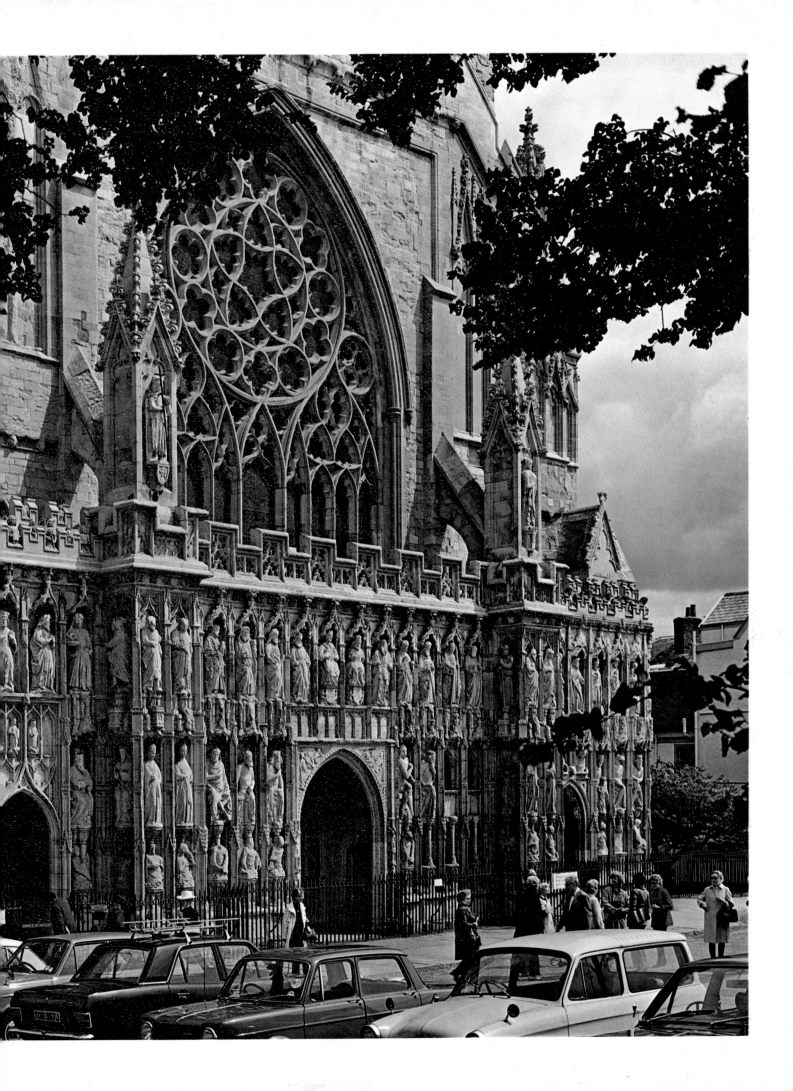

Hiding in the peace of Exeter Cathedral Close is this little gem of an Elizabethan house, one of the most perfect and interesting examples in the country. Known in Tudor times as 'Mol's Coffee House', it has been lovingly and carefully preserved and is still in use as a private house.

84

Jane Austen, who loved Lyme Regis, made The Cobb the setting of a memorable scene in *Persuasion* when her heroine Louisa Musgrove fell from its steps. She also gave a description of the little town which remains apt to this day :-

'The remarkable situation of the town, the principal street almost hurrying into the water, the walk to the Cobb, skirting round the pleasant little bay, which in season is animated with bathing machines and company, the Cobb itself, its old wonders and new improvements, with the very beautiful line of cliffs stretching out to the east of the town are what the stranger's eye will seek; and a very strange stranger it must be, who does not see charms in the immediate environs of Lyme, to make him wish to know it better.'

And so it still appears – apart from the bathing machines, for which, regrettably, now read 'caravans'.

West of the town is the celebrated Landslip where, in a tumble of rocks and gravel four miles long, the results of the effects of the erosive force of floodwater – not, for once, sea water – can be seen.

A jewel of a village on the edge of the Dorset Downs near Bridport, Powerstock has many places to interest the visitor. There is an ancient hill camp at Eggarden, a green mound which is all that remains of what was once King Athelstan's palace, and a superb old manor house at Mappercombe. The church in our photograph is St Mary's, which has two features of interest, an impressive 12th century Norman chancel arch with four rows of ornaments and a 15th century south doorway flanked by carved figures.

88

Strategically commanding a gap in the Purbeck Hills, Corfe and its castle have a history as old as that of England itself and as dramatic and bloody. It was here in Saxon times that King Edward the Martyr was murdered at his step-mother's behest. (Some of his bones may still be seen at Shaftesbury.) Here too were imprisoned and starved to death on King John's orders twenty French knights who were supporters of the murdered Prince Arthur. King Edward II, who was later murdered so obscenely in Berkeley Castle, was kept here secretly for months. During the Civil War the castle withstood repeated sieges until finally it was betrayed by one of its own garrison. It was blown up on Cromwell's orders but not very thoroughly, as can be seen here. The Isle of Purbeck is in reality a peninsula and is famous for its potter's clay and its marble-like building stone.

90

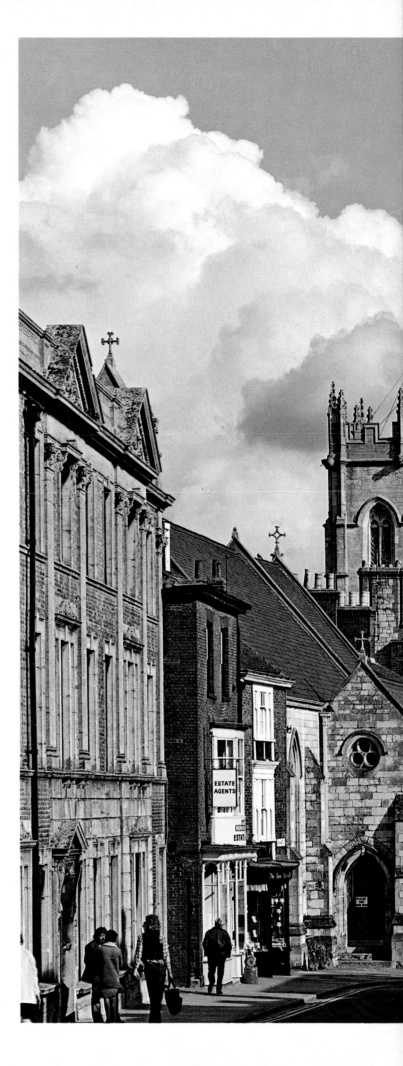

Dorchester, county town of Dorset and the 'Casterbridge' beloved of Thomas Hardy, has a history going back to the Stone Age and relics of its past are to be found scattered throughout the ancient town. At the Dorset County Museum is a collection of finds from the Iron Age fort at nearby Maiden Castle including the remains of defenders slain in battle with the Romans. The same museum also houses the Thomas Hardy Memorial Collection. In the council chamber there is a model of the ship *Mary and John* in which a party of Puritans, formed into a society by the Rev John White of St Peter's, Dorchester, sailed across the Atlantic to establish a church at Dorchester, Massachusetts. Opposite St Peter's Church in High West Street (on the left of our picture) is the house where the infamous Judge Jeffreys lived during the Bloody Assize when he sentenced 294 out of 300 Monmouth rebels to be hanged. The Judge himself now swings outside – his face on a shop sign.

A natural limestone archway in the cliffs to the west of the celebrated Cove at Lulworth. Lovers of Thomas Hardy's *Far from the Madding Crowd* will recall that Durdle Door is the place where Sergeant Troy swam out to sea on his fake suicide.

94

Looking across Chesil Bank from Abbotsbury at the western end to Portland Bill at the eastern. (The lighthouse guarding the treacherous Portland Race can just be seen). Between Chesil Bank and the mainland is a narrow stretch of water ten miles long called the Fleet. At Abbotsbury there is a celebrated Swannery — its hundreds of swans appear to 'own' the Fleet. Crowning the hill on the left of the picture is St Catherine's Chapel. Built of the same hard stone as Portland, it has walls over four feet thick and has withstood the elements for nearly five hundred years — a beacon and a look-out as much as a chapel.

The church of St Mary at Cerne Abbas seen on the left, is one of the most attractive in Dorset with a striking and beautifully preserved pre-Reformation Madonna and Child and superb fragments of 14th and 15th century stained glass as well as some 14th century wall paintings. Across from the church is a house where there once dwelt, it is said, an uncle of George Washington. On an adjacent hillside is that unmistakable fertility god, the Cerne Giant. He is 180 feet high and brandishes a club over a hundred feet long. The origins of the carvings are obscure. Some authorities believe it was a religious symbol going back before the Romans, others that it is of Saxon origin. The site now belongs to the National Trust. Modern scepticism tends to dismiss the time-honoured story that young ladies who walk over the appropriate parts of the carving are liable to unrequited motherhood.

Fiddleford lies on the edge of the fertile, tranquil Vale of Blackmore, on the banks of Dorset's chief river, the Stour.

102 Ashmore standing astride an old Roman road, is the highest village in Dorset with a superb view across Cranborne Chase to the Solent and the distant Isle of Wight.

Apart from its celebrated abbey, Milton Abbas has one of the most beautiful and intriguing village streets in England, identical cottages thickly thatched and each separated from its neighbour by a chestnut tree. It was built some two hundred years ago when John Damer, 1st Earl of Dorchester, bought the old village, pulled most of it down and built this new one at his gate. The houses are made of 'cob', a favourite building material in Dorset — a mixture of clay, slate and straw.

104

St Aldhelm (or St Alban) who gave his name to the forbidding limestone bluff 350 feet high between Swanage and Weymouth, was the founder and first bishop of Sherborne. The Abbey Church was then a cathedral and remained one for nearly 400 years. Inside it are the stone coffins of two Saxon kings Ethelbad and Ethelbert who succeeded each other and were succeeded in their turn by Alfred the Great.

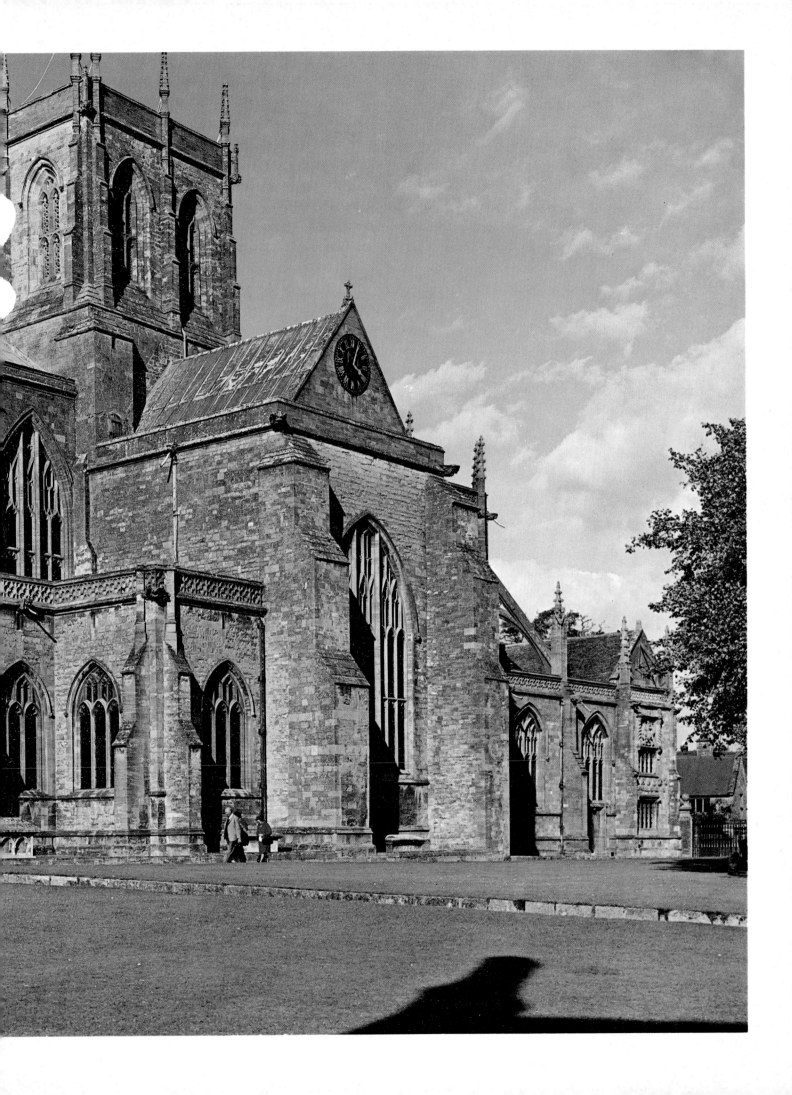

Shaftesbury, on its hill 700 feet up, looks out across the Vale of Blackmore, one of the gates to the real 'West Country'. Its celebrated abbey was founded by King Alfred – the Maker of the Nation – whose daughter was the first abbess. 'Gold Hill' is one of the increasingly rare cobbled streets in the West Country.

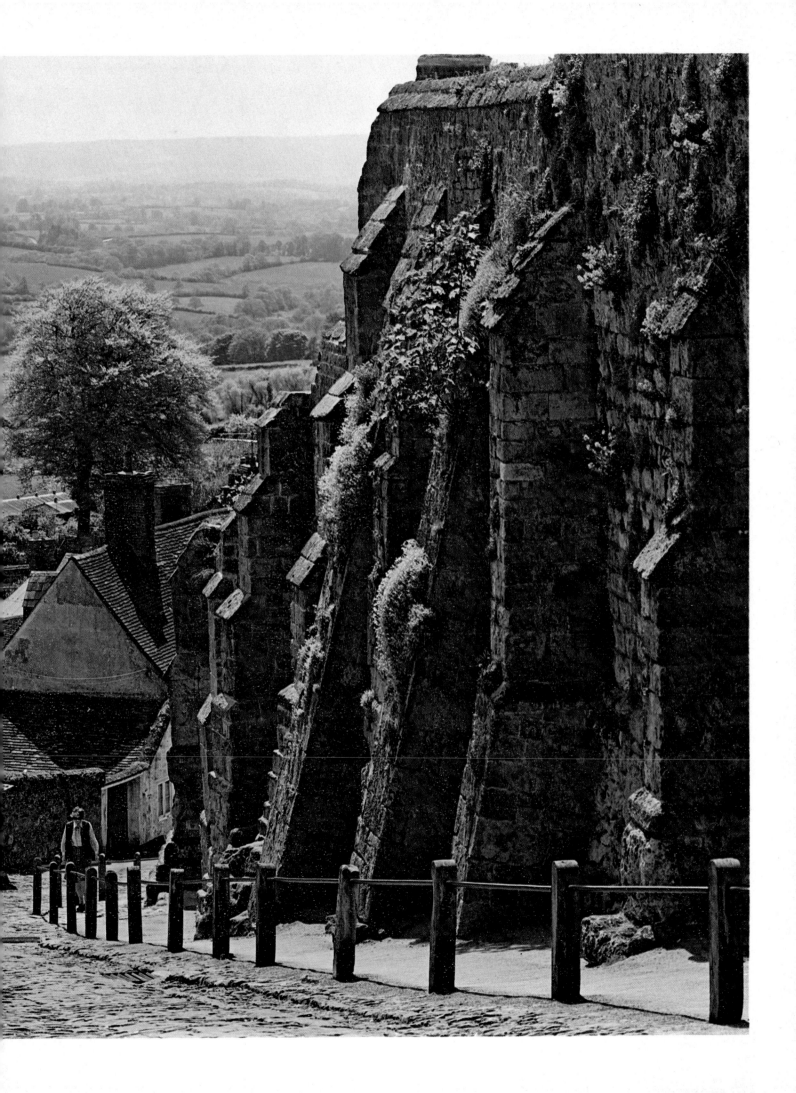

One of the most celebrated beauty spots on the Cornish coast, Kynance Cove's serpentine cliffs are beautifully veined and coloured. The curious shapes wrought by the sea and the vivid marking have given the individual rocks in the cove a variety of names like that of 'Asparagus Island', seen on the right of the picture.

110